D1545343

Houghton Mifflin
Reading
Indiana

Here We Go!

Senior Authors
J. David Cooper
John J. Pikulski

Authors
David J. Chard
Gilbert Garcia
Claude Goldenberg
Phyllis Hunter
Marjorie Y. Lipson
Shane Templeton
Sheila Valencia
MaryEllen Vogt

Consultants
Linda H. Butler
Linnea C. Ehri
Carla Ford

 HOUGHTON MIFFLIN   BOSTON

Cover illustration by Dave Clegg.

Acknowledgments begin on page 207.

Copyright © 2007 by Houghton Mifflin Company. All rights reserved.

No part of this work may be reproduced or transmitted in any form or by any means, electronic or mechanical, including photocopying or recording, or by any information storage or retrieval system without the prior written permission of the copyright owner unless such copying is expressly permitted by federal copyright law. With the exception of nonprofit transcription into Braille, Houghton Mifflin is not authorized to grant permission for further uses of this work. Permission must be obtained from the individual copyright owner as identified herein. Address requests for permission to make copies of Houghton Mifflin material to School Permissions, Houghton Mifflin Company, 222 Berkeley Street, Boston, MA 02116.

Printed in the U.S.A.

ISBN-13: 978-0-618-79683-0
ISBN-10: 0-618-79683-5

2 3 4 5 6 7 8 9 10 DOW 12 11 10 09 08 07

All Together Now

All Together Now

Realistic Fiction

Nonfiction

Poetry

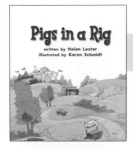

Surprise!

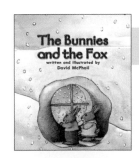
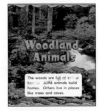

Surprise!

Realistic Fiction

Fantasy

Nonfiction

Read Together

All Together Now

Because we do
All things together
All things improve,
Even weather.

**from the poem "Together"
by Paul Engle**

Stories to Read

1 **Get Set Story**

Fantasy

2 **Main Story**

Realistic
Fiction

3 **Science Link**

Nonfiction

Words to Know

go   cat

on   sat

the

On the Go!

by Diane deGroat

13

Sam sat.

The cat sat.

Go, Sam!

Go, cat!

17

The cat sat on Sam.

Nadine Bernard Westcott has a cat named Lule. Whenever Mrs. Westcott draws in her studio, Lule naps nearby.

Mac the Cat

written and illustrated by
Nadine Bernard Westcott

21

Mac the cat is on the rug.

Mac the cat can tug and tug.

Mac the cat can get the ham.

Mac the cat can get the jam.

Mac the cat can see a hat.

Mac the cat sat on a bat.

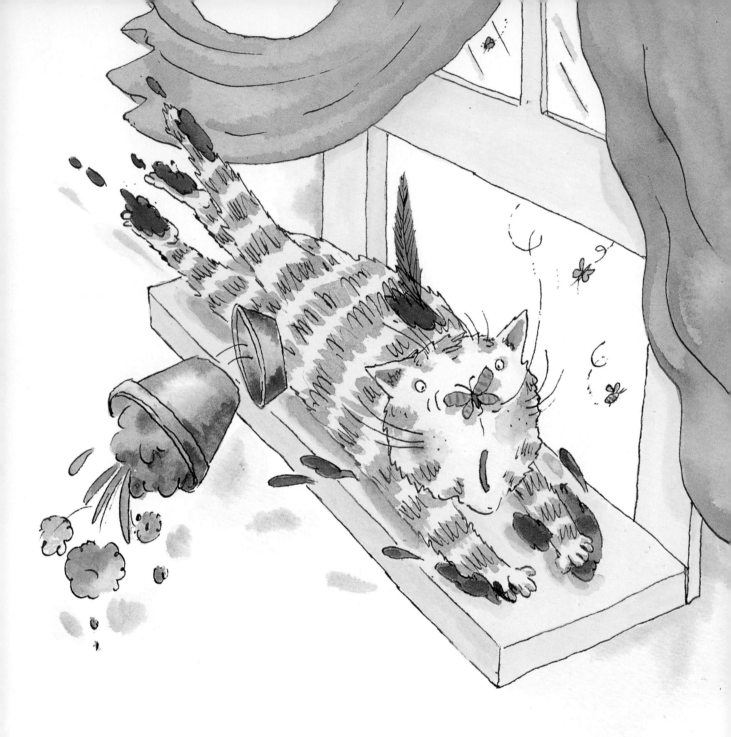

Mac can go and see a bug.

Mac can go and get a hug.

Shhh! Mac the cat is on my lap.

Mac the cat can have a nap.

Think About the Story

Mac the Cat

1 What did Mac get after he got the ham?

2 Why did the boy say "Shhh"?

3 What do you think Mac will do when he wakes up from his nap?

Retell the Story

Tell the story to a friend.
Use stick puppets.

 Writing ▶

Write a Label

Draw and label a picture of Mac.
Write about your picture.

Pet Cats and Big Cats

tiger

lion

Cats can be small, like pet cats. Cats can be big, like lions and tigers.

tiger cubs

pet cats

Cats play. Pet cats can play
with string. Tiger cubs can
play on the grass.

leopard

pet cat

Cats climb. The leopard can
go up a tree. The pet cat
can go up a tree, too.

pet cat

lion

Big cats are like pet cats.
They are all in the cat family.

Stories to Read

1 **Get Set Story**   **2** **Main Story**   **3** **Poetry Link**

Realistic
Fiction

Nonfiction

Poetry

Words to Know

and	can
here	fan
jump	nap
not	Pat
too	tap
we	

Cam and Pat

by Hector Borlasca

Cam can tap.
Pat can fan.

Pat can tap.
Cam can fan.

Cam can pat.
Pat can not.

42

We can pat.

Cam can jump here.
Pat can jump here, too!

44

Pat and Cam nap.

Meet the Author
When **Alma Flor Ada** was a child, her uncle and grandmother loved to tell her stories. Now she is a storyteller, too.

Meet the Photographer
Ken Karp started taking pictures when he was ten. He likes to take pictures of kids having fun.

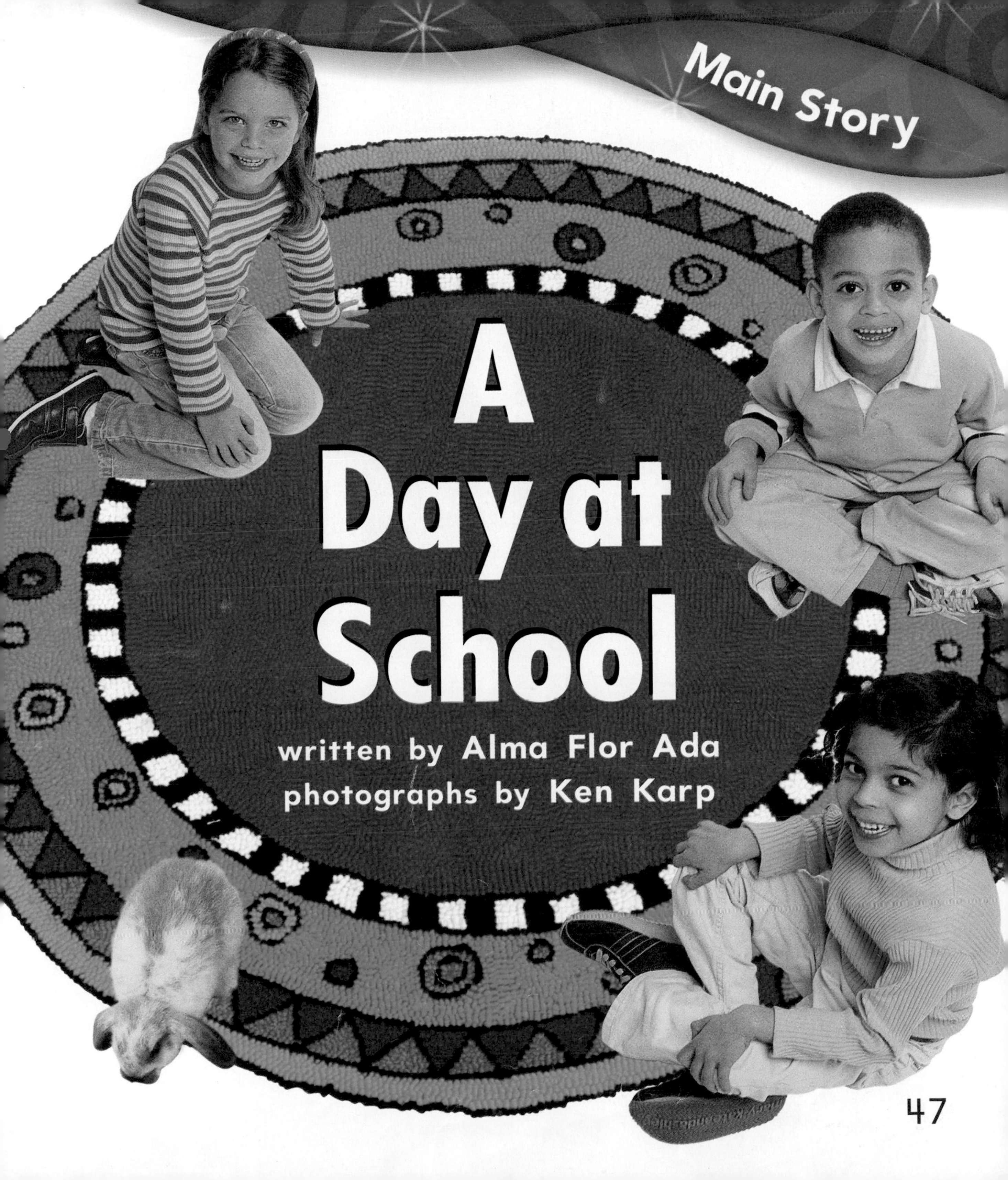

A Day at School

written by Alma Flor Ada

photographs by Ken Karp

Pam is at school.
Pam met the teacher.

We met Pam.

Pam sat here.
Pam can read.

Nat sat here.
Nat can read, too.

Pam can tap and sing.

We sing, too.

Pam can cut a fan.

Jen can cut a cat.

Pam and Nat can add.

Pam and Nat can add 3 + 2.

Pam, Nat, and Jen go to the playground.

Nat, Pam, and Jen play.

The pet can jump on Pam!
Pam can pat the pet.

The pet can not jump on Nat.
Nat let the pet have a nap.

We like school!

Think About the Story

A Day at School

A Day at School

1 What did the children do at school?

2 What did Pam and Nat do that is the same?

3 Would you like to go to Pam's school? Why?

Retell the Story

Act out the story with two classmates. Decide who will be Nat, Pam, and Jen.

Write a List

Make a class list of pets. Write "Our Pets" at the top of the list.

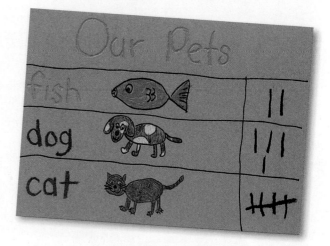

School

Wakes up early.
Just can't wait
to see who's coming.
Don't be late!

by Dee Lillegard

I Can

by Mari Evans

I can
be anything
I can
do anything
I can
think
anything
big
or tall
OR
high or low
W I D E
or narrow
fast or slow
because I
CAN
and
I
WANT
TO!

67

My Teacher

She loves fairy tales,
And poems,
And rocket ships,
And cream cheese,
And cotton candy,
And
ME!

by Kalli Dakos

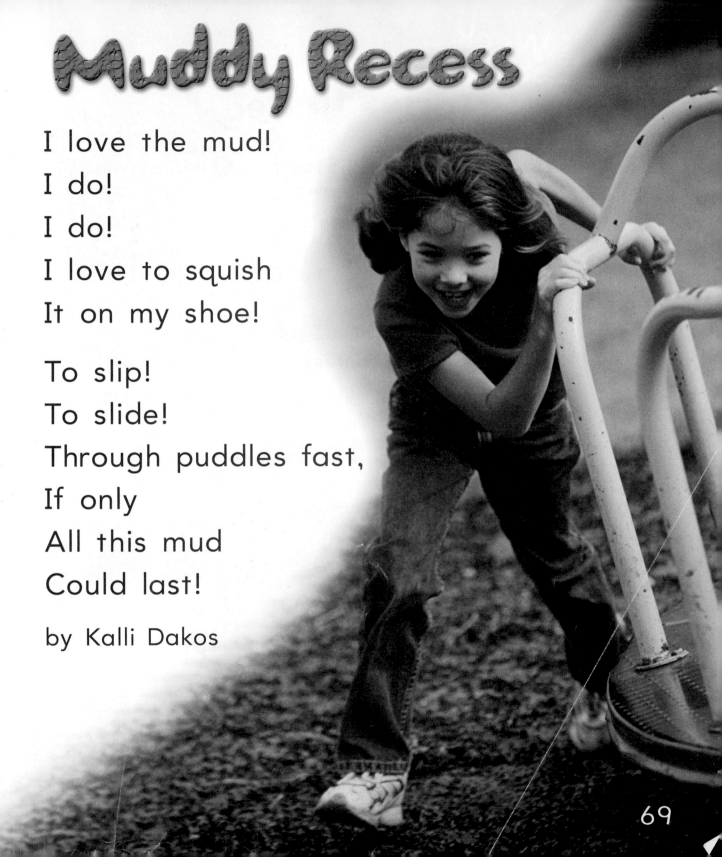

Muddy Recess

I love the mud!
I do!
I do!
I love to squish
It on my shoe!

To slip!
To slide!
Through puddles fast,
If only
All this mud
Could last!

by Kalli Dakos

69

Stories to Read

❶ Get Set Story

❷ Main Story

❸ Social Studies Link

Fantasy

Fantasy

Nonfiction

Words to Know

a	to	it
find	who	Pig
have	big	ran
one	hit	sit

A Big Hit

by James Williamson

Nan Pig can hit.

Sam Pig can hit, too.

Sam and Nan hit and ran.

Nan and Sam have to sit.

Fan Pig hit a BIG one!
Who can find it?

Nan and Sam can!

Meet the Author

Helen Lester was a teacher before she became an author. She likes to talk with children about books.

Meet the Illustrator

Karen Schmidt has illustrated over 30 books. Her favorite hobbies are hiking and skiing.

Helen Lester

Karen Schmidt

Pigs in a Rig

written by **Helen Lester**

illustrated by **Karen Schmidt**

Sid, Pal, and Fig sit in the tub.

Get in the rig.
Here we go!

Oops! The rig hit a big bump.
Goodbye to one pig!

Did Sid get in the mud?
Sid did get in it.

Oops! The rig hit a big pit.
Goodbye to one pig!

Did Pal find the jam?
Pal did find the jam.

Oops! The rig did a zig
and a zag.
Goodbye to one pig!

Can Fig fit in a bag?
Fig can fit in a bag.

We are a big mess!
We can fix the big mess.

91

We have to find the rig.
Who can see it?

We see the rig.
We ran to jump in.

Here we are.
Who can win?

Sid, Fig, and Pal win!
Goodbye!

Think About the Story

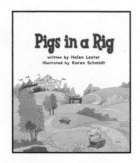

Pigs in a Rig

1 Which pig fell out of the rig first?

2 Why did the pigs go to the Pig Wash?

3 How would you keep the pigs from falling out of the rig?

Retell the Story

Draw a picture of your favorite story character. Use your picture to tell what happened in the story.

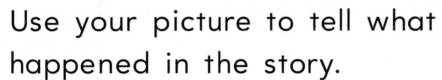

Writing

Describe a Character

Use punch-out letters to make a character's name. Write words to describe the character.

Let's Go to the Fair

Every year lots of people go to county fairs. Farmers bring their best animals for people to see.

It's fun to watch all the contests.
Dogs chase sheep. Horses pull logs.
Children hope one of their pigs or
lambs will win a blue ribbon.

People win prizes for their homemade pies and jam. There's even a prize for the biggest pumpkin!

You can have a fun day at a county fair!

Surprise!

No matter where I travel,
No matter where I roam,
No matter where I find
    myself,
I always am at home.

**from the poem "Riddle"
by Mary Ann Hoberman**

Stories to Read

1 Get Set Story **2** Main Story **3** Math Link

Fantasy

Realistic
Fiction

Nonfiction

Words to Know

five	two	got
four	upon	hot
in	what	lot
once	box	wag
three	did	

A Lot! A Lot!

by John Manders

One cat can wag.
Two got a pan.

Three cats fit
on a big can.

Four got in a box.

Five got hot, hot, hot.

What did we have?
A lot! A lot!

Meet the Author Angela Shelf Medearis writes books for children and grownups. She loves to cook big meals for her family.

Meet the Illustrator Nathan Jarvis has worked as an art teacher and a greeting card designer. He likes to ski and play tennis.

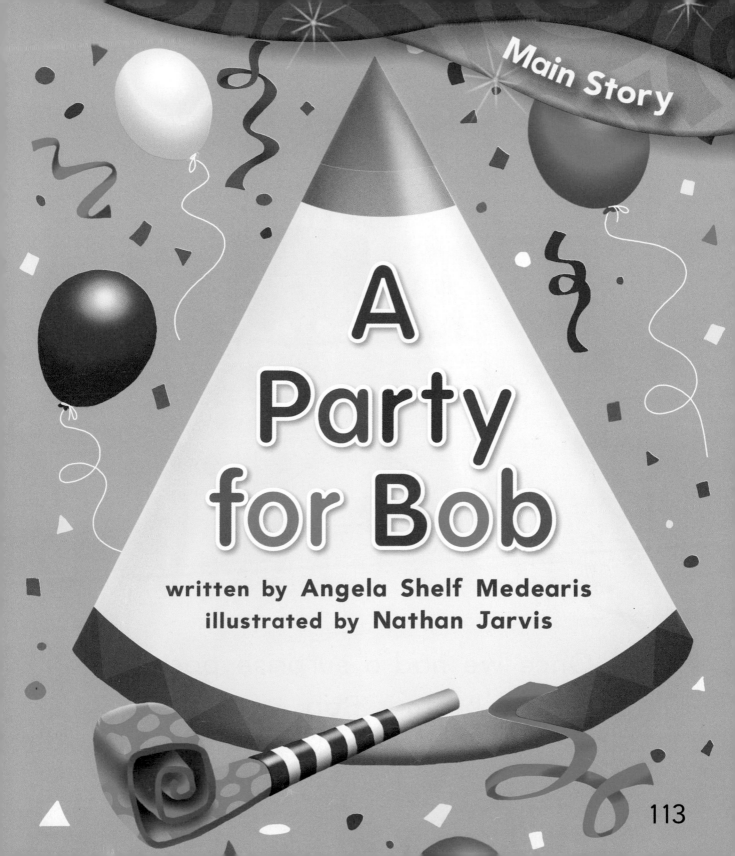

A Party for Bob

written by Angela Shelf Medearis

illustrated by Nathan Jarvis

Once we had a surprise party
for my brother Bob.
Here is what we did.

Mom and I got a big box.

Tom got here.
He had a gift for Bob.

Ben got here.
He had a wet gift.

Ben and Tom got in the box.
Two kids fit in the box.

Dot got here.
She had a big gift.

Dot got in the box.
Three kids fit in the box.

Tim got here.
He had a flat gift for Bob.

Tim got in the box.
Four kids fit.
Tim sat on Ben!

Wag and I had to
get in the box, too.

Five kids and Wag fit.
A lot fit in the box.
It got hot.

Tom, Ben, Dot, Tim, and I hid.
Wag hid, too.
Bob got here!

SURPRISE!

Mom lit six candles
upon the cake.

Happy Birthday, Bob!

Think About the Story

**A Party for
Bob**

1 How many kids fit in
the box?

2 Why did the kids hide?

3 What gift would you
bring if you went to
Bob's party? Why?

Retell the Story

How would Wag tell the story? Use a hand puppet of Wag to tell what happened.

Writing

Write a Sign

Make a sign for Bob's party.

Shapes Are Everywhere

Do you know what a triangle is?
A triangle is a shape that has
three sides, just like this half of
a sandwich.

A rectangle has four sides and four corners like this gift.

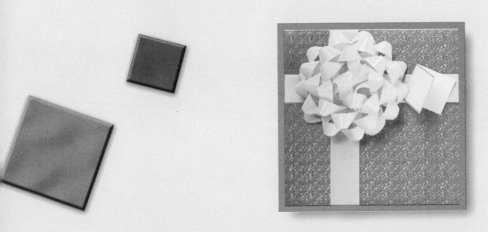

A square is a special kind of rectangle. All four sides of a square are the same, just like this gift.

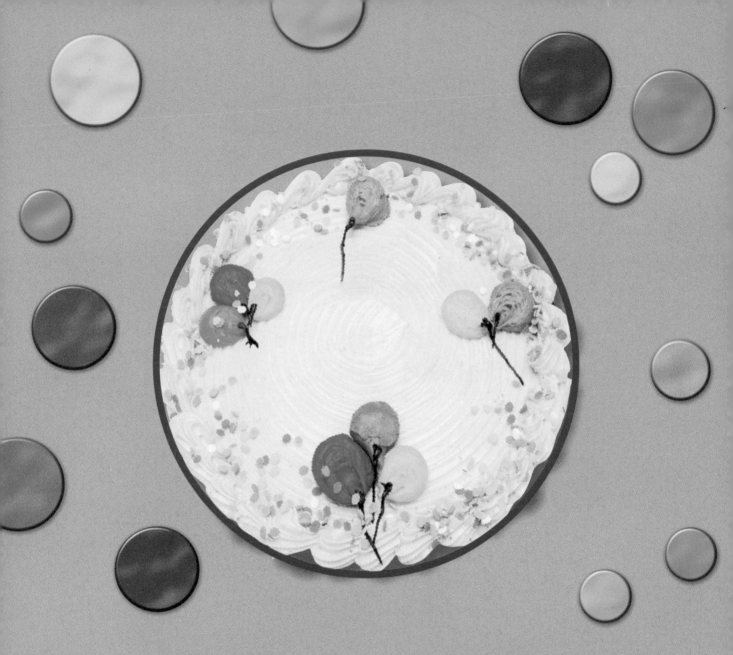

A circle does not have sides at
all! A circle is round like the
top of this cake.

Look at these pictures. What shapes can you find here?

Stories to Read

1 Get Set Story

Realistic
Fiction

2 Main Story

Fantasy

3 Science Link

Nonfiction

Words to Know

do	my	kid
for	said	next
I	you	yes
is	get	yet
me	help	

Val Can Help

by Elizabeth Sayles

Rob can not get it on top.
Can Val help him?

"I can help," said Val.
"I am a big kid."

"My hat is next to you," said Val.
"Can you get it for me?"

140

"Yes," said Rob.
"I can get it."

"I can not do it," said Rob. "Can you?"
"Not yet," said Val.

"You can help," said Val.
"You AND I can do it."

Read Together

Meet the Author and Illustrator

David McPhail has fun drawing
rabbits and other animals. He says,
"Ever since I could hold a crayon,
I have loved to draw."

144

The Bunnies and the Fox

written and illustrated by
David McPhail

Chapter 1

Kev and Viv are in the den.
"Can we play in the snow?"
said Viv.

"Not yet," said Mom.
"I can not let Fox find my
two kids."

"Is Fox bad?" said Kev.

"Yes, Fox is bad," said Mom.
"He can get you if you are little."

"Can Fox get Bear?" said Viv.
"Fox can not get Bear," said Mom.
"Bear is big."

"What if I am big?" said Kev.
"Can Fox get me?"

"Fox can not get you if you are
big," said Mom.

The little bunnies had a plan
for Fox.

Chapter 2

Kev said, "Can we play next
to the den, Mom?
We have a job to do."

"Yes," said Mom.
"If I see Fox, you can hop in
the den fast."

The little bunnies dug and dug.

"You two are wet," said Mom.

Kev and Viv sat and sat at
the window.
"Fox is here!" said Viv.

"Help!" said Fox.
He ran to the woods.
What did Fox see?

A BIG snow bunny!

"OK," said Mom. "Fox is not here."
"You can play in the snow."

Think About the Story

The Bunnies and the Fox

1 What did Kev and Viv do that real bunnies do not do?

2 Why did Mom tell Kev and Viv they could not play in the snow?

3 Do you think Fox will come near the bunny den again? Why?

Retell the Story

Work with a partner. Start at the beginning of the story. Take turns telling what happened.

 **Writing**

Write a Description

Draw your favorite part of the story. Write about your picture.

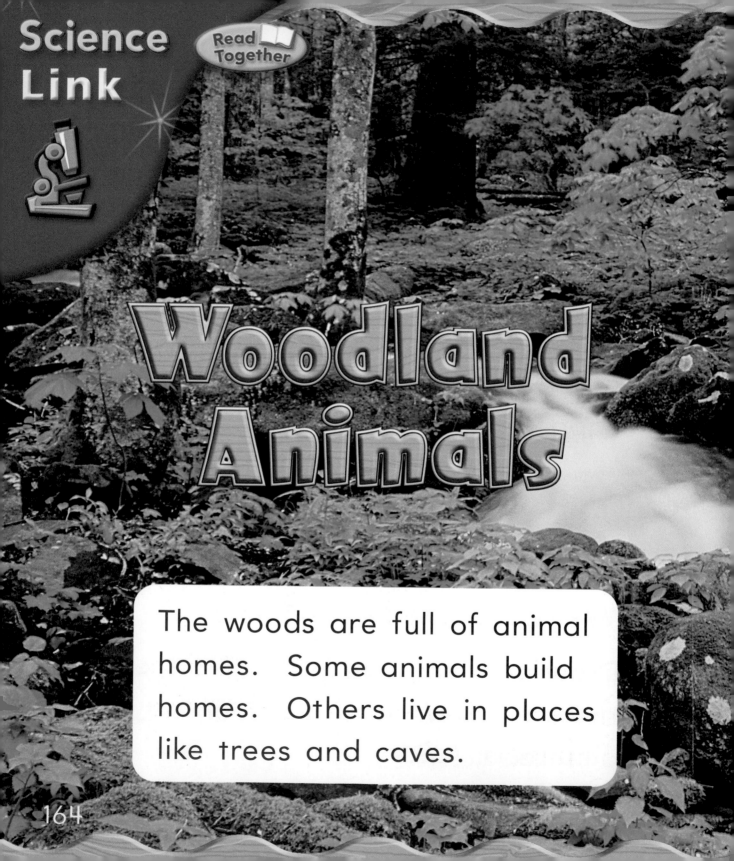

Woodland Animals

The woods are full of animal homes. Some animals build homes. Others live in places like trees and caves.

Foxes sometimes dig tunnels under the ground to make their dens. They store food in the tunnels, too.

Beavers cut down trees with their sharp teeth. They use the wood for building homes in ponds. A beaver home is called a lodge.

Porcupines often live inside trees. They have sharp quills that keep them safe from other animals. What other animals live in the woods?

Stories to Read

❶ Get Set Story

Realistic
Fiction

❷ Main Story

Fantasy

❸ Science Link

Nonfiction

Words to Know

are	pull	quit
away	they	up
does	where	zag
he	bug	zig
live	jug	

Quit It, Bug!

by Liz Conrad

Dan and Meg had a mat.
They set the mat on a log.

"Yuk!" said Dan.
"Get away, big bug!"

The bug did a zig and a zag
up the jug.

"Quit it, bug!" said Dan.
"Get the net!" he said.

"Pull up the mat, Dan," said Meg.
"Does the bug live in the log?"

Dan and Meg are on the mat.
Where is the bug?

Meet the Author
When **Pam Muñoz Ryan** is not writing books, she likes to take walks with her dogs Sami and Buddy.

Meet the Illustrator
Bernard Adnet illustrates books and game boards for children. He often uses a computer to create his drawings.

A Surprise for Zig Bug

written by Pam Muñoz Ryan
illustrated by Bernard Adnet

Here is Zig Bug.

"It is hot in my hut," said Zig.

"I see a pool," Zig said.

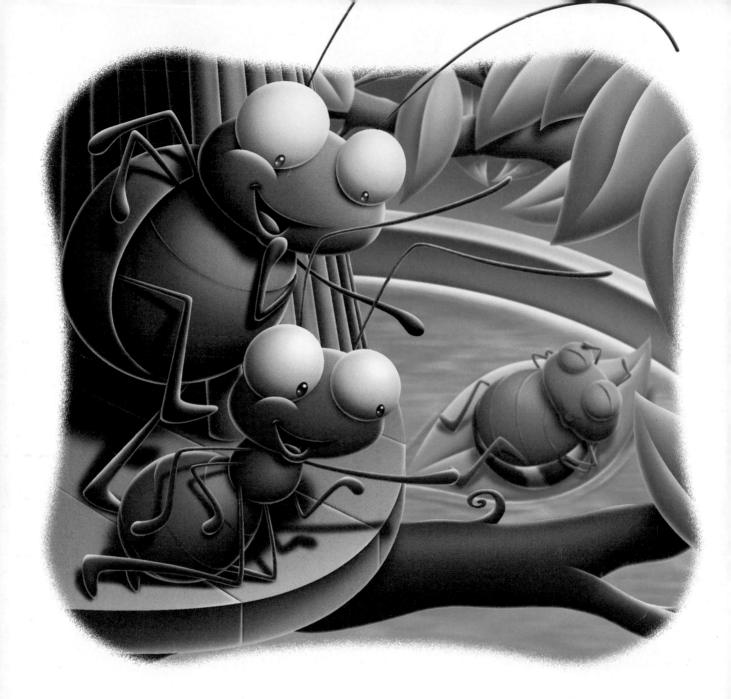

Kip Bug and Zag Bug live in a hut.
"I see Zig in a pool!" said Kip.

"Can we play?" Zag said.
"Yes, you can," said Zig.

"Away we go!"

Kip and Zag let go.
They get wet.

Zag, Kip, and Zig play in the sun.
They tug and pull.

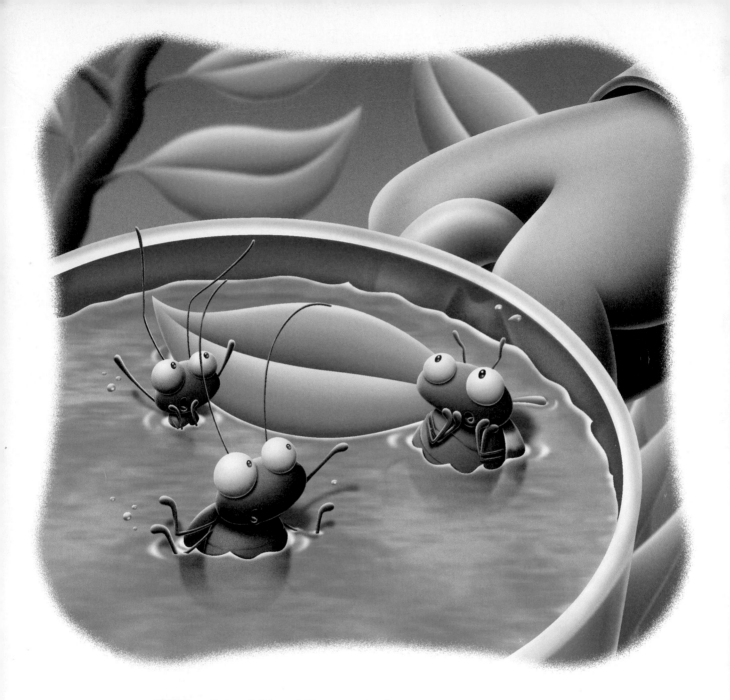

"Zig! Kip!" said Zag.
Kip, Zag, and Zig jump up.

"We are not in a pool," said Zig.
"We are in a jug!"

"Jump on my leaf!" said Zig.

"Away we go!"

Kip and Zag are in the mud,
but where is Zig?

Here he is!
Zig does not like mud.
He does not like the jug.

"I quit!" said Zig.

"We quit, too!" said Zag and Kip.

"We can sit in the hut."

192

"It is not too hot in here!"
said Zig.

Think About the Story

A Surprise for Zig Bug

1 What was Zig's problem at the beginning of the story? How did he solve it?

2 Why did the bugs land in the mud?

3 What do you think the bugs will do on the next hot day?

Retell the Story

Act out the story with two classmates. Decide who will be Zig, Zag, and Kip.

 Writing

Write a List

Make a list of other things Zig, Zag, and Kip might do together.

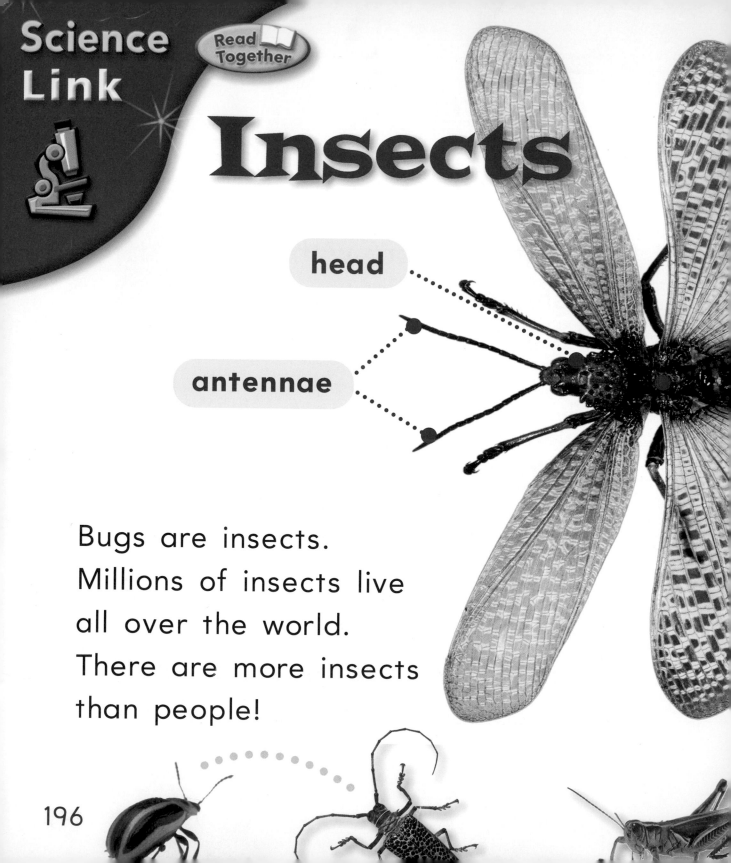

Read Together

Insects

head

antennae

Bugs are insects.
Millions of insects live
all over the world.
There are more insects
than people!

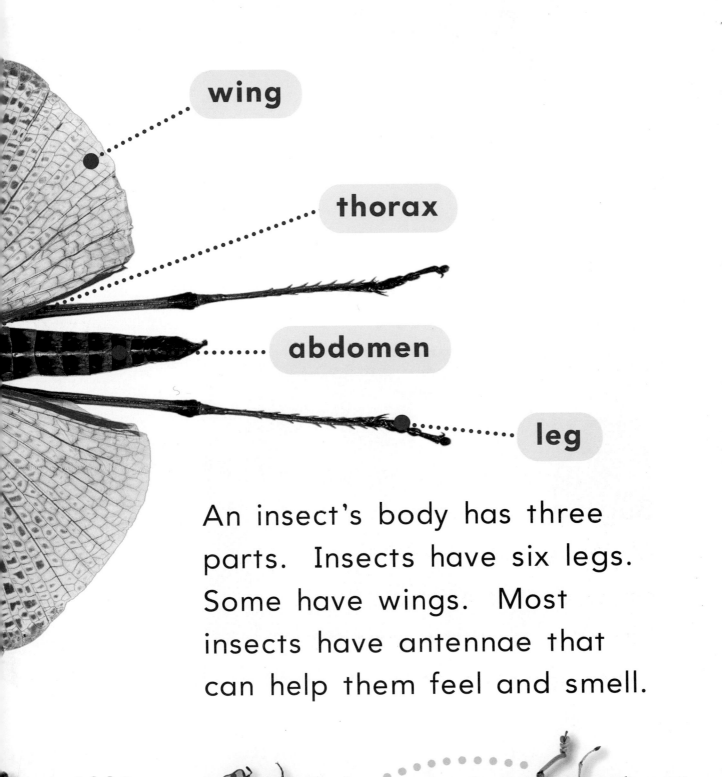

wing

thorax

abdomen

leg

An insect's body has three
parts. Insects have six legs.
Some have wings. Most
insects have antennae that
can help them feel and smell.

Some insects taste with their feet.

Some insects hear with their legs.

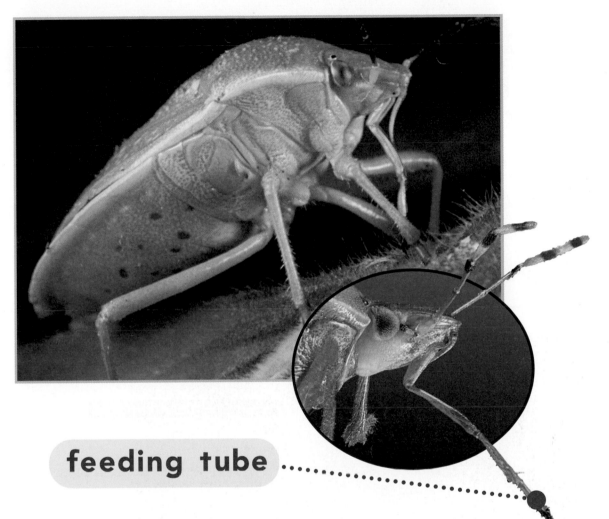

feeding tube

Some insects have special tubes
on the tips of their heads. The tube
works like a straw. The insect uses
the tube to suck up juicy meals.

Word Lists

On the Go!

DECODABLE WORDS

Target Skills:

consonants *m, s, t, c*
cat, Sam, sat

short *a*
cat, Sam, sat

HIGH-FREQUENCY WORDS

New
go, on, the

Mac the Cat

DECODABLE WORDS

Target Skills:

consonants *m, s, t, c*
cat, Mac, sat

short *a*
cat, Mac, sat

Words Using Kindergarten Review Skills
bat, bug, can, get, ham, hat, hug, jam, lap, nap, rug, tug

HIGH-FREQUENCY WORDS

New
go, on, the

Kindergarten Review
a, and, have, is, my, see

Cam and Pat

DECODABLE WORDS

Target Skills:

consonants *n, f, p*
can, fan, nap, pat, Pat, tap

short *a*
Cam, can, fan, nap, pat, Pat, tap

HIGH-FREQUENCY WORDS

New
and, here, jump, not, too, we

A Day at School

DECODABLE WORDS

Target Skills:

consonants *n, f, p*
can, fan, nap, Nat, pat, Pam, tap

short *a*
at, can, cat, fan, nap, Nat, Pam, pat, sat, tap

Words Using Kindergarten Review Skills
cut, Jen, let, met, pet

HIGH-FREQUENCY WORDS

New
and, here, jump, not, too, we
Kindergarten Review
a, have, is, like, play, to

Previously Taught
go, on, the

STORY VOCABULARY

add, playground, read, school, sing, teacher

A Big Hit

DECODABLE WORDS

Target Skills:

consonants *b, r, h, g*
big, hit, pig, ran

short *i*
big, hit, it, pig, sit

Words Using Previously Taught Skills
can, Fan, Nan, Sam

HIGH-FREQUENCY WORDS

New
a, find, have, one, to, who

Previously Taught
and, too

Pigs in a Rig

DECODABLE WORDS

Target Skills:

consonants *b, r, h, g*
bag, big, Fig, hit, pig, ran, rig

short *i*
big, Fig, fit, hit, in, it, pig, pit, rig, sit

Words Using Kindergarten Review Skills
did, fix, get, jam, Pal, Sid, win, zag, zig

Words Using Previously Taught Skills
can

HIGH-FREQUENCY WORDS

New
a, find, have, one, to, who
Kindergarten Review
are, see

Previously Taught
and, go, here, jump, the, we

STORY VOCABULARY

bump, goodbye, mess, mud, tub

A Lot! A Lot!

DECODABLE WORDS

Target Skills:

consonants *d, w, l, x*
box, did, lot, wag

short *o*
box, got, hot, lot

Words Using Previously Taught Skills
a, at, big, can, cat, fit, pan

HIGH-FREQUENCY WORDS

New
five, four, in, once, three, two, upon, what

Previously Taught
have, one, we

A Party for Bob

DECODABLE WORDS

Target Skills:

consonants *d, w, l, x*
box, did, Dot, had, hid, lit, lot, six, Wag

short *o*
Bob, box, Dot, got, hot, lot, Mom, on, Tom

Words Using Kindergarten Review Skills
Ben, get, wet

Words Using Previously Taught Skills
a, and, big, fit, flat, gift, it, sat, Tim

HIGH-FREQUENCY WORDS

New
five, four, in, once, three, two, upon, what

Kindergarten Review
for, he, I, is, my, she

Previously Taught
here, the, to, too, we

STORY VOCABULARY

birthday, brother, cake, candles, happy, kids, party, surprise

Val Can Help

DECODABLE WORDS

Target Skills:

consonants *k, v, y*
kid, Val, yes, yet

short *e*
get, help, next, yes, yet

Words Using Previously Taught Skills
a, am, and, big, can, hat, him, it, not, on,
Rob, top

HIGH-FREQUENCY WORDS

New
do, for, I, is, me, my, said, you

Previously Taught
to

The Bunnies and the Fox

DECODABLE WORDS

Target Skills:

consonants *k, v, y*
kids, Kev, Viv, yes, yet

short *e*
den, get, help, Kev, let, next, wet, yes, yet

Words Using Kindergarten Review Skills
dug

Words Using Previously Taught Skills
a, am, and, at, bad, big, can, did, fast, Fox,
had, hop, if, in, job, Mom, not, OK, plan,
ran, sat

HIGH-FREQUENCY WORDS

New
do, for, I, is, me, my, said, you
Kindergarten Review
are, he, play, see

Previously Taught
find, have, here, the, to, two, we, what

STORY VOCABULARY

Bear, bunny, bunnies, little, snow,
window, woods

Quit It, Bug!

DECODABLE WORDS

Target Skills:

consonants *q, j, z*
jug, quit, zag, zig

short *u*
bug, jug, up

Words Using Previously Taught Skills
a, and, big, Dan, did, get, had, in, it, log, mat, Meg, net, on, set, yuk

HIGH-FREQUENCY WORDS

New
are, away, does, he, live, pull, they, where

Previously Taught
is, said, the

A Surprise for Zig Bug

DECODABLE WORDS

Target Skills:

consonants *q, j, z*
jug, jump, quit, Zag, Zig

short *u*
Bug, but, hut, jug, jump, mud, sun, tug, up

Words Using Previously Taught Skills
a, and, can, get, hot, in, it, Kip, let, not, on, sit, wet, yes

HIGH-FREQUENCY WORDS

New
are, away, does, he, live, pull, they, where

Kindergarten Review
like, play, see

Previously Taught
go, here, I, is, my, said, the, too, we, you

STORY VOCABULARY

leaf, pool

HIGH-FREQUENCY WORDS TAUGHT TO DATE

a	here	said
and	I	the
are	in	they
away	is	three
do	jump	to
does	live	too
find	me	two
five	my	upon
for	not	we
four	on	what
go	once	where
have	one	who
he	pull	you

Decoding skills taught to date: consonants *m, s, t, c;* short *a;* consonants *n, f, p;* consonants *b, r, h, g;* short *i;* consonants *d, w, l, x;* short *o;* consonants *k, v, y;* short *e;* consonants *q, j, z;* short *u*

Acknowledgments

Main Selection

A Surprise for Zig Bug, by Pam Muñoz Ryan. Copyright © by Pam Muñoz Ryan. Published by arrangement with the author.

Poetry

"I Can" from *Singing Black,* by Mari Evans, published by Reed Visuals. Copyright © 1979 by Mari Evans. Reprinted by permission of the author.

"Muddy Recess" from *Mrs. Cole on an Onion Roll and Other School Poems,* by Kalli Dakos. Copyright © 1995 by Kalli Dakos. Reprinted with the permission of Simon & Schuster Books for Young Readers, an imprint of Simon & Schuster Children's Publishing Division.

"My Teacher" from *Mrs. Cole on an Onion Roll and Other School Poems,* by Kalli Dakos. Copyright © 1995 by Kalli Dakos. Reprinted with the permission of Simon & Schuster Books for Young Readers, an imprint of Simon & Schuster Children's Publishing Division.

"Riddle" from *The Llama Who Had No Pajama: 100 Favorite Poems,* by Mary Ann Hoberman. Copyright © 1973, 1998 by Mary Ann Hoberman. Reprinted by permission of Harcourt, Inc.

"School" from *Hello School: A Classroom Full of Poems,* by Dee Lillegard. Text copyright © 2001 by Dee Lillegard. Reprinted by permission of Alfred A. Knopf, an imprint of Random House Children's Books, a division of Random House, Inc.

"Together" from *Embrace: Selected Love Poems,* by Paul Engle. Copyright © 1969 by Paul Engle. Reprinted by permission of Random House, Inc.

Credits

Photography

3, 5 © PhotoDisc/Getty Images. **7, 8** © Steve McAlister/The Image Bank/Getty Images. **10–11** © Jim Cummins/Corbis. **11** (m) PhotoDisc/Getty Images. **32** Fredde Lieberman/Index Stock Imagery. **34–37** (border) Anthony Bannister/Gallo Images/Corbis. **34** (tr) Patricia Doyle/Stone/Getty Images. (ml) DigitalVision/PictureQuest. (mr) Tom McHugh/Photo Researchers, Inc. **35** (r) © Tom & Pat Leeson Photography. (l) G. K. & Vikki Hart/The Image Bank/Getty Images. **36** (r) Alan Carey/Photo Researchers, Inc. (l) John Foxx/Creatas. **37** (r) © Terry Whittaker/Photo Researchers, Inc. (l) Yann Arthus-Bertrand/Corbis. **46–63** © HMCo/Ken Karp. **46** (tl) Courtesy of Alma Flor Ada. **64** Photodisc/Getty Images. **66** (inset) Gary Russ/Getty Images. (bkgd) Michael Newman/PhotoEdit. **67** Lisette Le Bon/SuperStock. **68** Eyewire Productions/Getty Images. **69** Anton Vengo/SuperStock. **96** Photodisc/Getty Images. **98** border images listed from left to right, (1) Burke/Triolo Brand X/PictureQuest. (2) G. K. & Vikki Hart/PhotoDisc. (3) C. Squared Studios/PhotoDisc. (4) G. K. & Vikki Hart/PhotoDisc. (5) Burke/Triolo Brand X Pictures/PictureQuest. (6) G. K. & Vikki Hart/PhotoDisc. (7) C. Squared Studios/PhotoDisc. (8) G. K. & Vikki Hart/PhotoDisc. (9) Siede Preis/PhotoDisc. (10) C. Squared Studios/PhotoDisc. (11) G. K. & Vikki Hart/PhotoDisc. (m) Wayne Eastep/Getty Images. **98–99** (bkgd) Patrick Ward/Corbis. **99** (tl) Richard A. Cooke/Corbis. (tl-inset) Phil Schermeister/Corbis. (br) Kelly Beck/Corbis. **100** (tl) David Young-Wolff/PhotoEdit. (bl) Dennis Gottlieb/FoodPix. (r) Larry Lefever/Grant Heilman Photography. **101** (t) Bob Krist/Corbis. (b) American Images/Superstock. **102–103** © Jim Brandenburg/Minden Pictures. **103** (m) © Steve McAlister/The Image Bank/

Getty Images. **130** Photodisc/Getty Images. **132** Kathryn Russell/FoodPix. **133–134** C Squared Studios/PhotoDisc/Getty Images. **135** (tl) Burke/ Triolo/Brand X Pictures. (tm) Rick Gayle/Corbis. (tr) C Squared Studios/PhotoDisc. (m) Jim Linna/ PhotoDisc/Getty Images. (bm) Burke/Triolo/ Brand X Pictures. **162** The Image Bank/Getty Images. **163** © HMCo/Ken Karp. **164–165** (bkgd) William Manning/Corbis. **165** (t) PhotoDisc Collection/Getty Images. **166–167** (bkgd) William Manning/Corbis. **166** (tl, mr) John Swedberg/Bruce Coleman. **167** (tr) Ron Sanford/Corbis. (ml) John Foster/Masterfile. **194** Getty Images. **195** © HMCo/Ken Karp. **196** (bl) Bob Anderson/Masterfile. (bm) Davies & Starr/Stone/Getty Images. (br) Darlyne A. Dr. Murawski/National Geographic/Getty Images. **196–197** (m) Davies + Starr/The Image Bank/ Getty Images. **197** (bl, br) Barbara Strnadova/ Photo Researchers. **198** (tl) Photodisc Collection/ Getty Images. (tr) Anthony Bannister/Gallo Images/Corbis. (m) Michael & Patricia Fogden/ Corbis. (bl, bm) Barbara Strnadova/Photo Researchers. (br) Davies & Starr/Stone/Getty Images. **199** (tl) George D. Lepp/Corbis. (mr) Darwin Dale/Photo Researchers. (bm) Darlyne A. Dr. Murawski/National Geographic/Getty Images. (br) Bob Anderson/Masterfile.

Illustration

12–19 Diane deGroat. **20–31** Nadine Bernard Westcott. **38–45** Hector Borlasca. **70–77** James Williamson. **78–96** Karen Schmidt. **104–111** John Manders. **112–129** Nathan Jarvis. **136–143** Elizabeth Sayles. **144–162** David McPhail. **168–175** Liz Conrad. **176–194** Bernard Adnet.